All of a sudden, Haden sat up in bed.

"What's that?" he whispered. "It sounds like a rocket landing in the street."

What's That Sound?

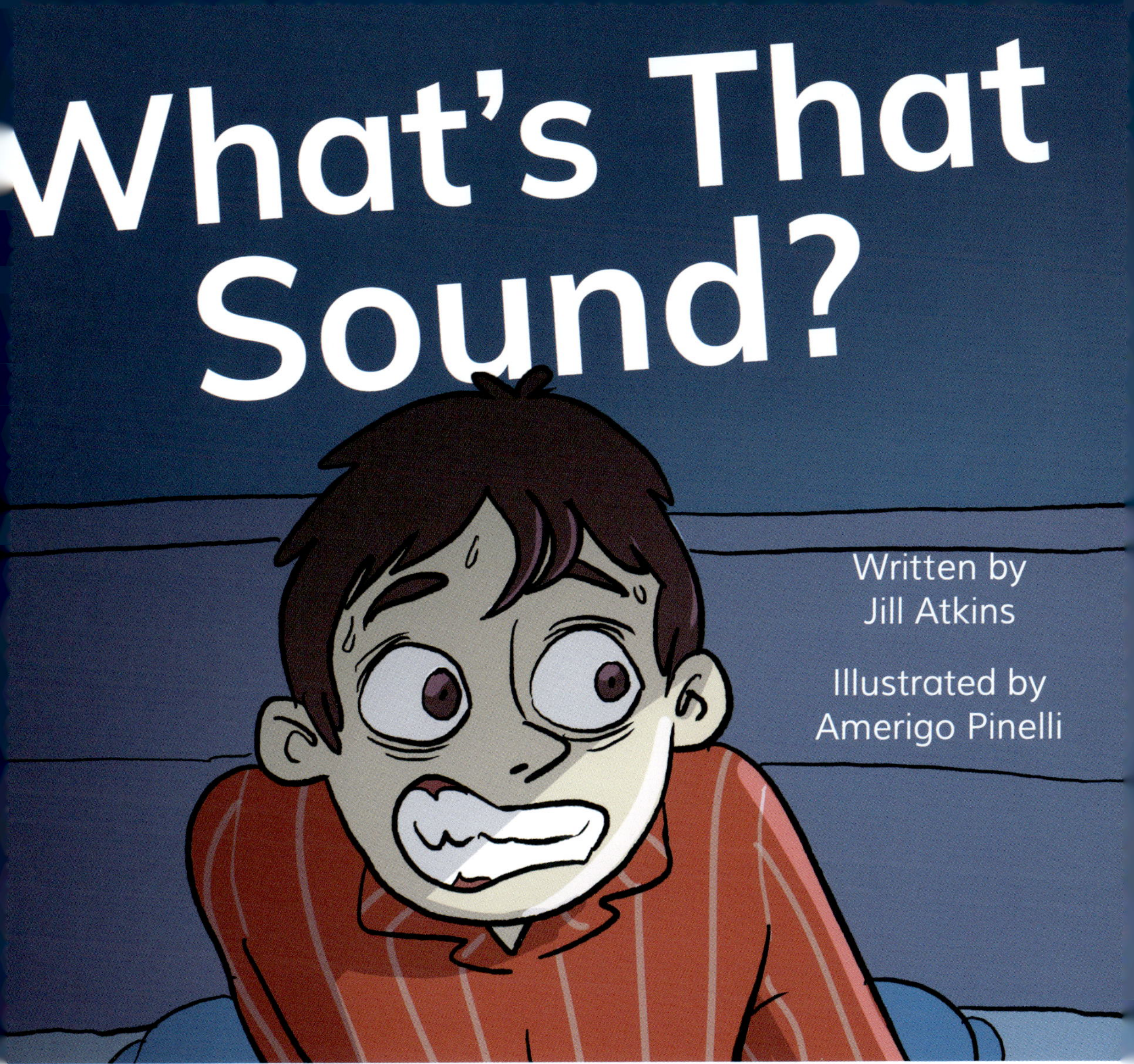

Written by
Jill Atkins

Illustrated by
Amerigo Pinelli

Published in 2026 by
Norwood House Press
2544 Clinton Street
Buffalo, NY 14224

Printed in the United States of America

Library of Congress Cataloging-in-Publication Data:
Names: Atkins, Jill (Children's author). | Pinelli, Amerigo, illustrator.
Title: What's that sound? / written by Jill Atkins, illustrated by Amerigo Pinelli. Lemurs / by Jill Atkins.
Description: Buffalo, NY : Norwood House Press, 2026. | Series: Phonics all-stars: phase 5b
Identifiers: ISBN 9781978578746 (pbk.) | ISBN 9781978578753 (library bound) | ISBN 9781978578760 (ebook)
Subjects: LCSH: Reading–Phonetic method–Juvenile literature. | English language–Phonetics–Juvenile literature. | Sounds–Juvenile fiction. | Sleepovers–Juvenile fiction. | Lemurs–Juvenile literature.
Classification: LCC LB1573.3 A796 | DDC 372.465–dc23

CPSIA compliance information: Batch #CW26NHP: For further information contact Norwood House Press at 1-800-237-9932.

It was well past midnight.

Haden lay in bed in the darkness. Asif and Joe were on the carpet in their sleeping bags.

It had been a fun night. They had cooked bacon and eggs, and then played some games outside.

“No way,” said Asif. “It’s just a car revving.”

Haden frowned, but he stayed in bed where he felt snug.

Haden tried to get to sleep, but it was no good.

"What's that?" he asked. "It sounds just like a rocket landing in the street."

"You're so dramatic," said Joe. "It's just a plane landing at the airport."

Haden didn't think that was right, but he didn't argue.

The third time Haden sat up, he was positive he was right.

"Didn't you hear that?" he asked. "That's such a racket. It **must** be a rocket landing in the street."

Asif snickered. "It's just someone playing the drums," he said.

Haden sighed and had a sip of water. Asif and Joe were now starting to annoy him.

As he lay back in bed, Haden's ears were filled with the same sound.

What was it? Where was it?

"You've got to be not hearing it," he said. "I'm telling you, it's a rocket landing outside in the street."

"No way!" said Joe. "It's a jackhammer."

A bit later, Haden still insisted.

"A jackhammer?" he said. "Where, at this time of night?"

Then Haden paused. The racket was getting louder.

"I'm positive that's a rocket landing in the street," he said.

"Well, I'm positive it isn't!" shouted Joe. "It's a train jamming on its brakes."

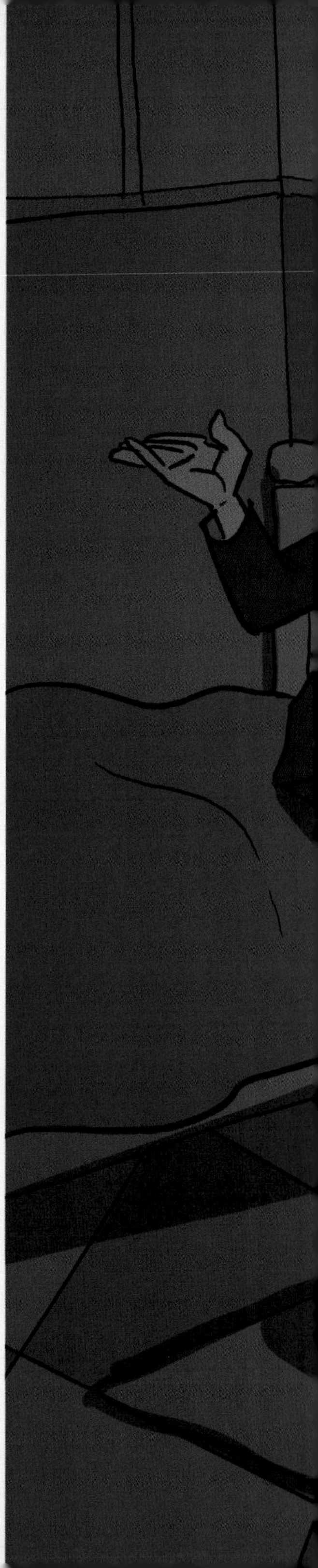

"Let's just look outside," said Asif.

They felt their way across the room in the dark. Asif ripped back the curtains.

"See!" said Haden. "I was right!"

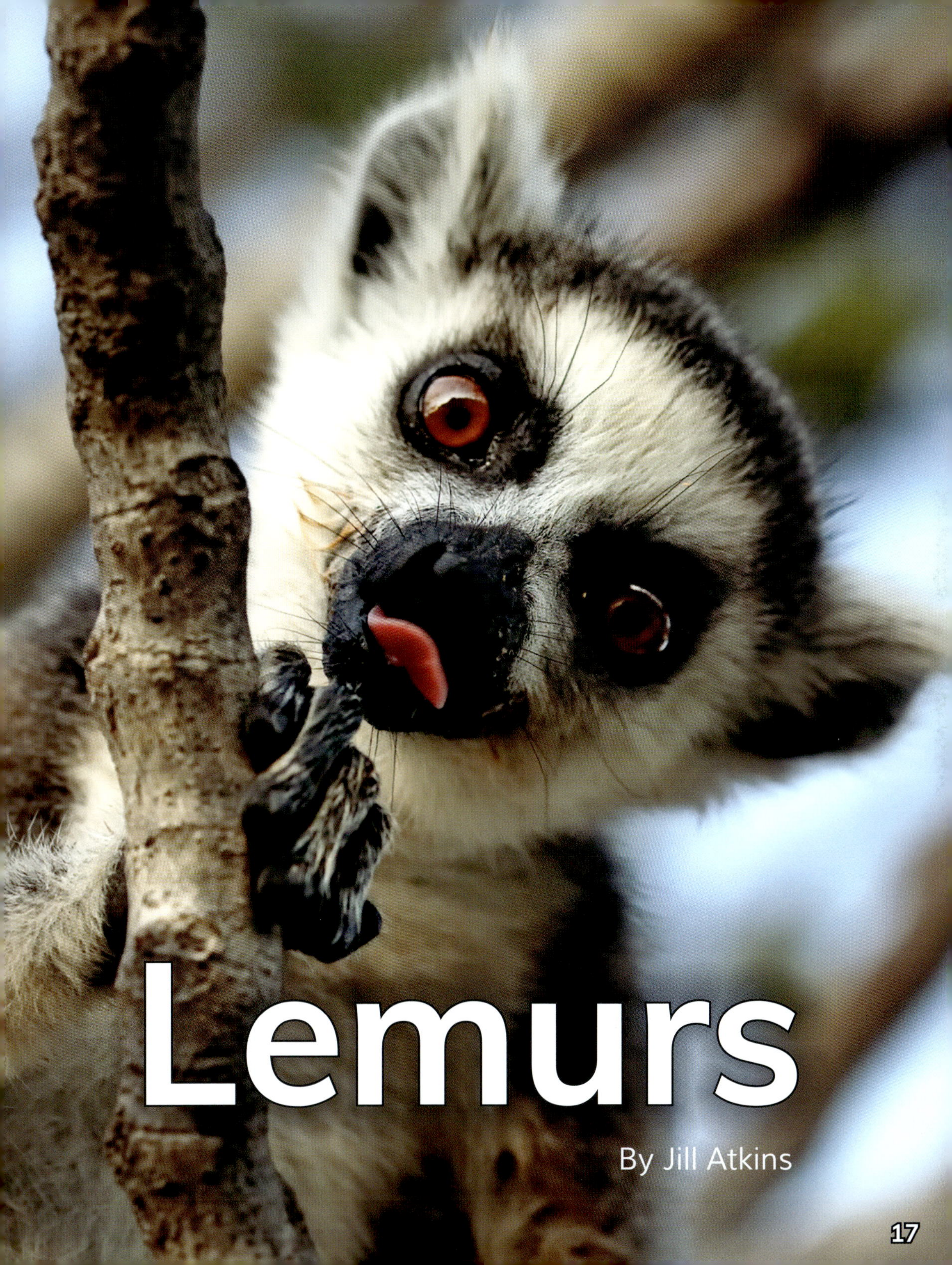

Lemurs

By Jill Atkins

Lemurs come from Madagascar, which is just off the east coast of Africa.

Lemurs inhabit the thick forests of Madagascar.

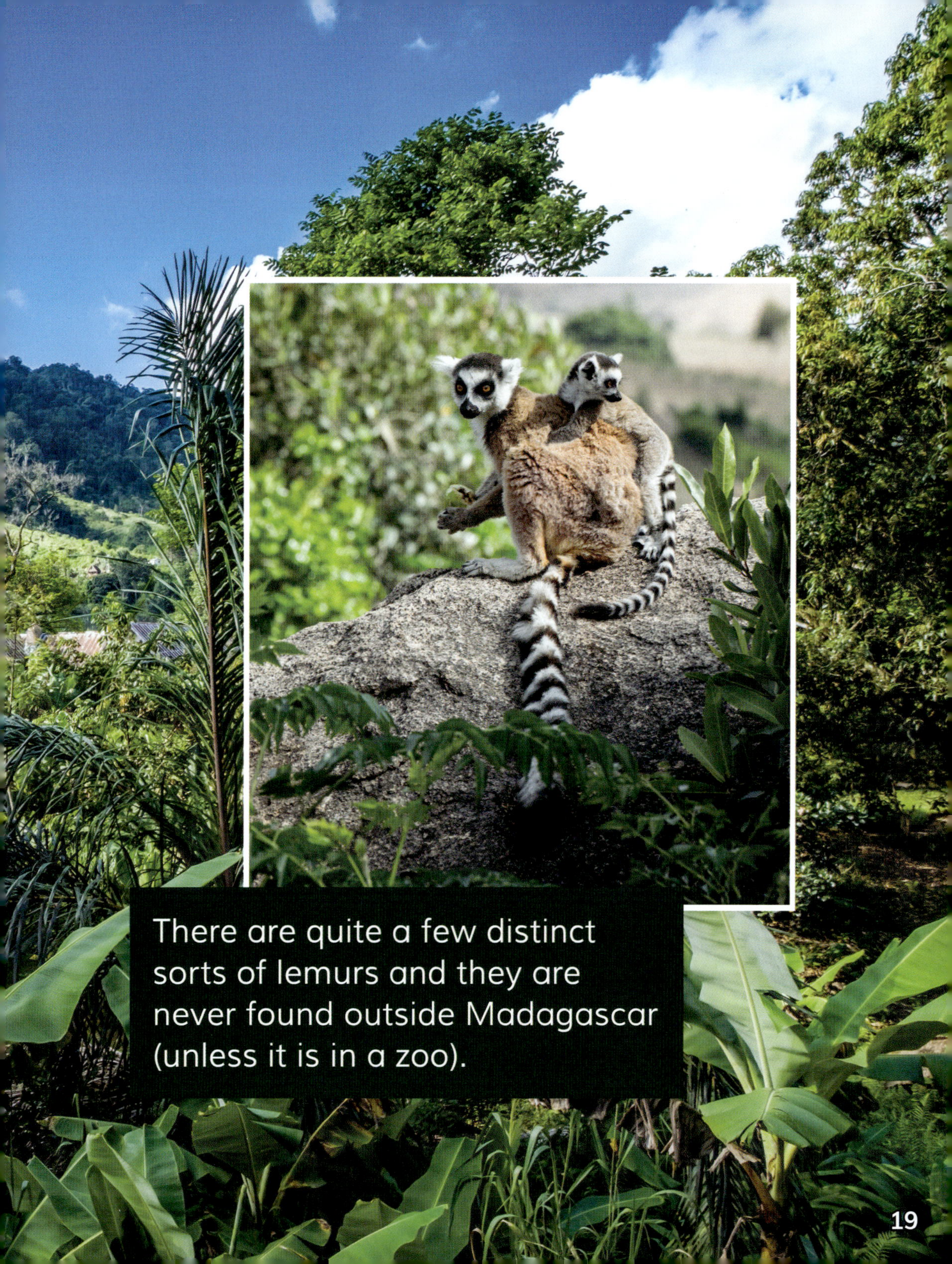

There are quite a few distinct sorts of lemurs and they are never found outside Madagascar (unless it is in a zoo).

A lot of lemurs have soft, pale brown fur, long, wet snouts and pointed ears.

Their tails are long, but it's the rings on the tail that we think of when we read about lemurs.

However, not all lemurs have rings on their tails – or pointed ears, for that matter.

Lemurs can leap from tree to tree, but they are quick on the ground as well.

With their tails held high, they look as if they are having fun.

The lemurs' tails help them stay upright when they leap, run and hop.

When the lemurs are on the ground, their tails act as a signal to the rest of the lemurs, so they do not get lost.

A crowd of lemurs is not called a squad or a bunch. It is called a troop.

The dominant lemur in a troop – the boss – will be a female. Even her female offspring will be the boss of all the male lemurs.

A troop of lemurs likes to stay clean, so all the members of the troop get washed and groomed.

In the daytime, lemurs wander around in the forest, looking for food.

Then, at night, a troop sleeps all together in the trees.

Sometimes, ring-tailed lemurs will sleep in caves. They will return to the same cave to sleep again and again.

The number of lemurs in Madagascar is now in decline.

Their habitat is vanishing, as there are people who want to cut down or burn the forests.

As the trees disappear, it is harder for the lemurs to get the food that they need.

People who have seen lemurs say that they are so cute to watch.

If you see ring-tailed lemurs at the zoo, you might want to go back again and again.

Maybe the lemurs like watching you, as much as you enjoy looking at them.